Dan and Kathy.

To those who ho
learning and a love o
happy reading!
Warmest regards,
Todd

MATCHING WITS

A collection of poetry by
F. Willis Keene and Todd Keene

Prologue

Before the telephone, before electricity, ball point pens, typewriters, the telegraph, or any other modern means of communication or conveying one's thoughts, the goose quill or lead pencil ruled our universe. In this simpler time, the men and women of letters were seemingly less encumbered by outside influences and free to express themselves by their own devices. I often imagine exactly what my great grandfather had in mind when he penned some of the loveliest words I've read, though he makes his point quite clearly.

In my earlier life, I was drawn to the written word without truly knowing what pulled me to it. Nor did I know why my prose was more flowery or of an earlier day than my classmates. I simply wrote what I sensed deep inside of me, blind to my influences. That is, until something great was revealed to me.

It happened one day when my aunt presented me with a book of my great grandfather's writing. I read it with amazement. It included poems about nature, love lost or love found, the passing of loved ones, and heartfelt expressions of one's devotion to God and love interests. My great grandfather spoke to me as though he were in the room with me, which, after further pondering, I am quite convinced he was and is.

His work, mostly in pencil, includes crossed out words and re-writes, giving a glimpse as to his line of thinking as he was writing. One such piece, a poem about the four seasons, was never truly finished. I brazenly took the liberty of finishing it for him and felt a mysterious hand guiding me in the process. I think he would be pleased with the finished product.

This book is a compilation of the writings of my great grandfather, F. Willis Keene, side by side with my own work on the same subjects. It also includes my own efforts at children's poetry, inspired by the birth of my nephew, Andrew.

Some of the pieces between F. Willis and mine seem eerily familiar to each other, though in fact I had never read even one of his poems when I crafted mine. Despite the century and a half gulf between our writings, we are mysteriously and inexplicably bonded. I've grown to admire F. Willis for his great depth of expression. In this book, I hope that the modern reader can get to know him as well.

F. Willis had many notable friends and family members. His brother, John Keene, was a brilliant orator, having delivered the masters oratory at his alma mater, DePauw University in Greencastle, Indiana. John was an early contributor to the founding of Aetna Life Insurance, and F. Willis was involved in the firm as well, when his writing could wait. The Keene's can trace their lineage back to King Edward I of England, also known as Edward Longshanks, and even further back to Rollo (Gaange Rolf), the first Duke of Normandy.

I am eternally grateful to a man I have never met, yet feel that I've come to know quite well. Thank you, F. Willis, for the legacy you've left the Keene Family, and to you, Dear Reader, for breathing life into this extraordinary man.

ISBN-13: 978-0-578-72912-1

Designer: Avery Eddy
Cover Photographer: Michael Koch
Project Manager: Emily Potts

Dedication

This book is dedicated to my wife, Vicky, my one and only muse for my musings on love. It is dedicated to my parents, Walter and Barbara, who encouraged me from an early age to express myself in writing, and who supported my endeavors as an actor on stage. It is dedicated to my sisters, Jill and Erin, who, with Vicky, remain my best friends and greatest supporters. It is dedicated to my Aunt Nelda Keene, who compiled the works of F. Willis and, perhaps without knowing it, fostered my idea for this book. It is dedicated to my Uncle Carl Goembel and Aunt Margaret Goembel, who have encouraged my writing at every step, and to my late grandparents, Howard and Florence Keene, and Carl and Helen Goembel, whose love is ever present. It is also dedicated to my daughter Amy, her husband Thom, and her children, Vivienne, Aslan, Una, Livia, Caruso and Ivy Wyn.

I am grateful to my family and friends, to the grace of God, and for the many gifts He has bestowed upon us. Blessings to you, and happy reading!

Contents

ON NATURE

Lines on the Reception of a Bouquet

Kind nature in so many forms,
Hath shown itself sublime;
With garbs mysterious and complete,
With beauty quite divine.

And in the little lovely flow'r,
Its beauties fair are seen;
With sundry colors, shapes and forms,
In loveliness supreme.

And now allow me to express
My feelings here and say,
That I receive with happiness,
This priceless gem bouquet.

And shall esteem and treasure it,
In sweeter thoughts of thee,
Who cull'd it from sweet nature's bed,
And styled me the donee.

— *F. Willis Keene*

Nature's Grand Surprise

Petals dance is soft warm winds
A pastel morning to begin
Fields of pink and red and blue
Reflected in the summer's hue

Sunbeams signal the grand parade
Sublimely lighting nature's way
A day to behold the life so dear
Of precious moments captured here

The joys revealed once to explore
Where splendid meadows and streams adorn
Ne'er more hidden, the discovery landed
A secret solace, a mind expanded

A pageant, a spectacle, a grand surprise
Nature's love through wondrous eyes

— *Todd Keene*

The Seasons

We have in winter, frost and snow,
Bleak chilling winds, which fiercely blow,
And weather cold-severe,
'Tis then we see all shrubs and trees
So desolate and bare of leaves,
And every thing so drear,
But when cold blasty winter's o'er
And snow and frost is seen no more,
In comes the verdant spring,
With many pretty open'ng flowers,
And also sweet refreshing showers,
And merry birds do sing
The sprightly lark and cooing dove,
In songs that seem to reach above,
To God are giving praise;
The black boblink, and mocking bird,
The martin too -- yes all are heard,
To warble their sweet bays,
And when the summer doth come in,
We have warm weather to begin,
And many thunder showers;
'Tis then those forest trees are seen,
Completely clad in foliage green,
Which shows God's mighty pow'rs,
The ripening wheat, and growing corn,
Do every where, the fields adorn,
And make the farmer glad,
Cherries and berries of all kind,
Apples and other fruits combin'd,
Are gathered by the lad,
But soon the autumn will appear,
With biting frosts which farmers fear,
And nights and mornings cool,

Then on the flowers and the trees,
"Jack Frost" will force their dropping leaves,
But first in fields once summer green,
Fall's splendor emerges in colors seen,
Afore the branches, desolate and bare,
Winter's grasp doth chill the air,
And now the seasons one and all,
The winter, spring, summer and fall,
Thus ever pass away,
Briefly noted by quill this day,
Nature's grandeur, resplendent and complete,
Its loveliness in full, is striven to portray.

— *F. Willis Keene*

ON LOVE

An Acrostic

Felicity with joy and mirth,
O! may you share, while on this earth;
Replete with ev'ry earthly bliss,
May he who rides the stormy skies;
In all respects the world defies,
Serenely smile on thee, dear miss.
Sun and moon, the orbs of light,
Kind nature proves for day and night;
Also for seasons, warm and cool,
The stars which deck the spacious heav'n,
Elemental orbits are giv'n;
With their sphere, each one to rule,
Each orb of light, is quite sublime,
But still, thy charms are more divine;
Standing paramount, supreme,
Thy every look imparts thy grace;
Each tranquil smile adorns thy face,
Resplendently divine, serene.

— *F. Willis Keene*

God's Masterpiece

For Vicky,
June 23, 1999

With brush and palette
God's masterpiece created
In color and in contrast
Fair beauty He fabricated

Curved and subtle
This canvas in human form
Bountiful spirit and blessed heart
So delicate and warm

Blessed am I to know
This work of art so pure
The very best of nature
With love that shall endure

More splendid than the petal
That stems from flower yon
More beautiful with each day
From thence to well beyond

And on this hallowed eve
The anniversary of our years
Four and ever counting
God's grace brings joyous tears

— *Todd Keene*

An Acrostic II

For thee I now take up my pen,
On this pale sheet my mind rehearse,
Requesting thee to not condemn,
My thoughts portrayed in humble verse,
Incompetent though I do feel;
Such charms as thine, to here essay;
Sweet justice yet with loud appeal;
My thoughts direct, and says/portray;
A bright impression of thy form,
Reflects in beauty on my mind,
Thy ev'ry look in fancy's charm,
Hath prov'd itself serene divine.
And while in fancy's path I stray,
Charms alluring prospective rise.
Radiating like Lord of day;
Unchanged magnetic like it flies,
Perfect peach, and earthly bliss,
Pleasure too, without allay;
Each day may prove your happiness;
Replete at last, with heavenly joy.

— *F. Willis Keene*

For Vicky

Your hair is soft this day
My how it glows
To touch it now is Heaven
Heaven surely knows

Your eyes are green and gray
All full of knowing
They see beyond all earthliness
And peer into my soul

If your ears were listening now
And heard my every sound
Through muted lips, I'd whisper how
I love you more each day

— *Todd Keene*

An Acrostic III

'Tis sweet to muse and pen a line,
On moments spent with thee;
Could I but half my thoughts define,
On such felicity;
Unfeigned I am in all I say;
Sweet justice prompts me thus portray,
Indeed those sparkling, eyes of thine,
No sunshine can excel;
Serene and calm, thy ways divine,
Unmatched, unparalleled,
Stars and moon may brightly shine,
And yet thy smiles are more sublime,
No distance, time, nor even space,
Can dim or cloud this theme;
Hence, the charm of thy sweet grace,
Is standing paramount, supreme,
Now may each earthly pleasure sweet,
Ne'er fail to prove thine own replete.

— *F. Willis Keene*

Vicky Through a Lens

Portraits and pictures
Your soft glowing features
Canvas and camera
The captured reminders

Tell of the beauty
As seen through the eyes of
The lens and the artist
And all who survey

And so you know that
To be near you
To know you
Is a treasure in itself

So much concealed
What a lens cannot reveal
The magic, the heart of, the beauty of
You.

— *Todd Keene*

An Acrostic for Cousin Mary

These lines cousin Mary I write for you,
On kindred love, affection too;
Cajolery not known;
O, may each earthly pleasure sweet,
Unspeakably prove your replete,
Such earthly bliss be shown,
I hope while on this earth you live,
Nothing but peace you will receive,
May God impart His grace,
And let His love, true and divine,
Resplendently on thee to shine,
Your troubles to erase,
Forever to enjoy His love,
Replete it last with Him above,
Eternal joys be giv'n;
No earthly pain can enter there,
Celestial joys then may you share
High up in sweet heaven.

— *F. Willis Keene*

Vicky, Peace and Harmony

Alone with you
I feel such peace and harmony
Inside of me
Like an ocean's wave that sets you free
It carries me
And flows upon the current in my mind
I'm lost in time
And everything is beautiful
For all I see is you
All I see is you

— *Todd Keene*

To Miss —

Dear lady, when I view thy face
My heart is filled with thy sweet grace —
I cannot help esteem thee.

Thy sparkling eyes of pretty blue,
A waving hair of auburn hue
Completely enamor me.

Thy gentle step and graceful form,
Have in themselves a lovely charm,
Saccharinely sweet.

Thy rosy cheek and marble neck,
With beauty fair will ever deck,
And make your charms complete.

— *F. Willis Keene*

And She's There

Love is what you find
On the way to somewhere else
Distracted and torn
We put our lives on a shelf
As we toil upstream
There's just no time it seems
For the important things
It's all just so bland
Each day is the same
Always a flicker
But never a flame
Until the moment it happens
Until the earth stands still
Until the planets align
And the stars are upon us
And she's there
Where the air is rare
Where nothing is a care
Where the night is ours to share
And forever's just coming clear
Because she's there

— *Todd Keene*

Come on Home

Out of love
Out of time
Out of patience
Out of line
In our moments
In our time
In our fury
In our crime
Once so beautiful
Once sublime
Once to hold you
Once so fine
Here I am to offer me
Here I am to hear your plea
Oh so fragile
Oh so dear
Oh to hold you oh so near
Supplications hard to render
In relations once so tender
All our feelings
Returned to sender
Come on home love, come on home
All's forgotten and forgiven
No words on which to dwell
Let's get on now with the living
Let's create our new Heaven
Come on home, come on home
Sweet love, come on home.

— *Todd Keene*

ON FAMILY

To the Memory of My Mother

Ho, thou are gone! my mother dear,
And bid a last adieu;
Now shrouded in the silent grave,
Excluded from my view.
Those eyes which once beheld me here,
Are closed in endless night;
Thy precious form is snatched away,
Forever from my sight.
Thy lovely voice, so sweet to me,
No more will greet my ears;
But pain and grief attend me now,
While I'm bedew'd with tears.
Oh! if this all were but a dream,
How happy I should feel;
But death, alas! upon thy brow,
Hath set his signet seal!
I've seen thee borne upon thy bier,
And, oh, the deep-toned bell
Struck on my heart, in pensive notes,
Thy solemn fun'ral knell!
Could I but say and feel it too,
I knew not grief nor pain;
Could tears or words or wail of woe,
Restore thee back again.
But now, thou art gone home to Christ,
To live on earth no more;
But dwell with Saints in endless bliss,
On Canaan's happy shore.
Yes, now thy body's in the tomb,
And spirit's gone to rest;
Housed in with God - forever his,
And numbered with the blest.
Now father, do not weep I say,

Although dear mother's gone!
She's left this world of grief and gloom,
For that bright heav'nly bourne.
The wound is deep, I feel the sting!
It pierces me with pain;
But, father rest assured, our loss
Is her eternal gain.
And brothers, do not grieve and mourn,
Dear Mother now is blest;
She's with the angel band on high,
In Jesus' sweet arms at rest.
And with our angel Sister now,
Where tears are ever dry;
She's looking out for us to come,
With ever watchful eye.
She now is freed from earthly cares,
No more to grieve and sigh;
But, rest in realms of perfect love,
And peace with God on high.
There shine far more resplendently,
With the heav'nly host;
And ever bless God's holy name,
For having saved the lost.
There walk Jerusalem's golden streets,
And praise for ever more,
The Father, Son and Holy Ghost,
On that celestial shore.

— *F. Willis Keene*

Poem for Dad, Walter W. Keene

There are men
And there are princes
With crowns worn ahigh
Anointed not of self
But placed by One on high

To be esteemed and ever treasured
They seek not self-glory
Nor earthly want or need
But to share their love completely
To serve and nurture thee

The highest form of human kind
These humble princes be
Deserving one's greatest praise
Exalted and lauded
For love personified

Such blessings are the greater men
With spirits beyond compare
Father, friend and husband
By any name a joy
A beautiful soul is he

Life enduring forevermore
God shines upon this man
For warmest thoughts evinced
Immeasurable it seems
No mere man, a Heavenly prince!

— *Todd Keene*

Inscription Upon My Father's Tombstone

Farewell to you my sons, my stay with you is ended,
My soul has left its clay, and with your Mother's blended,
In life she was my joy, we worshipped God together,
In death our souls are one, with praise to Him forever.
To you we now are looking, with every watchful eye,
In blest anticipation, to join us by and by,
Weep not for us we ask you, from all your grief refrain,
Your loss, which is but earthly, is our eternal gain.

Peoria, 1873

— *F. Willis Keene*

For My Father

Sometimes I feel like
It's me against the world
Frightened, torn awhirl

The pieces of me still
Have fight enough to kill
This growth inside of me

And how it grows!
Whose will would doth betray
My every waking day?
Is it right for me to say
God help my demon slay?

Life, in the fullest measure
I strove, to do your pleasure
Lord, I'm yours and you must know
Even the good must someday go

But not too soon for me I hope
I've struggled just to cope
Endured most every scope
Administered by man

You've kept me here this long
Through pain, you've made me strong
Can it be your solemn wish
For my life, to prolong?

I've served you to my best
Through your gifts I confess
And never missed a chance
To be your faithful man

Sometimes I feel like
It's me against the world
Lord, through you might I be cured
Returned to health, secure

Free to be myself,
To dance, perchance to dwell
In heaven here on earth
Oh! might I see
The wonder of rebirth

— *Todd Keene*

Dedication to the Caregivers of My Father

For the angels we have here on Earth
Ever seeking our rebirth
Nurturing our every need
Where we hurt and where we bleed

I owe you a debt I never can repay
I'm at a loss, except I'll say
My days you brighten in every way
Kindness follows each word you say

The simple touch of your hand
Reaches the depth of me
And not so fleeting as the sands
Oceans of love, wide as the sea

I pray for you, I pray for me
I pray for us all on bended knee
For the many, many lives you save
For those you've lost through struggle brave

Angels surely walk among us
For God has made it thus
This I know, I've seen it true
I've seen His love that pours through you

Please know I'm indebted beyond measure
And mere words can never express
How much I sincerely treasure
Your abundant love and kindness

With profound gratitude and thanks,
Todd Keene and Family

— *Todd Keene*

Forget Me Not When I Am Gone

(Composed by Sarah F. Keene two weeks previous to her death)

I often think, when on my couch,
Of friends now passed away;
Some of them my dear school mates,
With whom I once did play
Where are they now? I ask;
They're gone to bliss or woe,
To the dark regions of the dead,
Where we must shortly go.
We've seen their faces for the last,
In this vain world of care;
But, if we reach that happy place,
We hope to meet them there.
Soon as our bodies are conveyed,
Into that lonely grot,
So soon, my friends, we all do know,
That we shall be forgot.
But when I leave you all my friends,
To seek that lonely spot,
It is my wish, my sincere wish,
Never to be forgot.

— *Sarah F. Keene*

Poem for Dickory

Whenever your heart needs to mend
And the happiest songs have left your head
Forget all the things left unsaid
The moments you wish you could have spent
Remember the one you called friend
And know that the world's without end

Climb to the star that lights your world
And see your universe yet unfurled
Take all the joy that you can know
Paint your horizon all aglow
Give all the love that you can send
And know that the world's without end

Celebrate this force of life
It flows eternal through you and I
He'd contend you shan't lament
For this journey has no end
Dream your dreams of love and then
Know that the world's without end

Life might seem unfairly brief
When this earth is all you see
You're blessed and you must know
Someday there's a light he will show
It will guide you on your way
He's just ahead of us this day

Love is a never ending song
Words and music shall play on
A melody within your heart
On your soul it shall impart
Wondrous joy shall sing to you

And carry forth forever through
Whenever your heart needs to mend
Know that the world's without end

Read at the funeral for Dickory Rudduck, Sydney, Australia, June, 2013

— *Todd Keene*

To the Memory of My Sister

My dearest sister little thought,
While penning the above;
That she would hear the call so soon,
From Him who speaketh love;
To yield to death's relentless hand,
While in the bloom of youth;
And enter vast eternity,
No more return to earth!
But soon it was the summons came,
While with her kindred near,
Yet, far from home, from brothers watch,
And parents tender care,
The cruel icy hand of death,
Snatch'd her so soon away,
To stand before the judgment bar,
And meet the judgment day!
And now she's far from this bleak earth,
Where peace is vainly sought;
Into that country, far from view,
Unpierc'd by human thought
Where peach and love do ever dwell,
And reigneth endless bliss;
Where grief and sorrow enter not;
But all is happiness.
Leaving father, mother, brothers,
And friends to mourn and weep
While is housed in paradise,
In Jesus' arms to sleep.
Yes, now no doubt she's with her God,
To ne'er depart again;
But live rejoicing on His sight,
Freed from all care and pain,
Her closing verse - the last she made,

I never shall forget;
Till I alike am call'd from earth,
To pay the final debt.
She said that "when she left her friends,
To seek that lonely spot,
It was her wish, her sincere wish,
Never to be forgot"
And now though many years have passed,
Since she was call'd to rest,
Yet, she is bright in mem'ry still,
While sorrow fills my breast.
How could I e'er while life remains,
Forget my sister dear,
Who nursed me when a little babe,
With love and tender care.
No time dear Sis, one thought of thee,
Can from my mind erase,
Me thinks I now can hear your voice,
And see your smiling face.
Though time may in its speedy course,
Some things erase from mind,
Yet thou wilt every dearly be,
Around my heart entwined.

— *F. Willis Keene*

All Must Die

How many a gallant knight and maid,
Have in the clay cold earth been laid,
And from their friends and land they trod,
Been call'd away to meet their God!
And infants too, by that dreaded death,
Been forc'd to yield their mortal breath,
And torn from their dear mother's breast,
Thou within the silent tomb to rest!
The sceptered king, the slave, the proud,
The vile and meek, must wear a shroud;
And clods of earth lie o'er their breast,
Now doomed to their eternal rest.
The wise, the brave, the great, the small,
The rich, the poor; yes one and all,
Without a doubt must surely die;
And in the damp and cold grave lie!
Yes all things living on this earth,
Must die, as sure as they have birth;
'Tis God's command they must obey,
And from this earth be ta'en away
And when we view the wax-like dead,
Lying beneath the coffin li;
We can't forbear to sob and cry,
And realize that shortly we must die,
The proof of death is stronger still,
For thus we find, it is God's will;
For "dust thou art," through Christ we learn,
"And unto dust shalt thou return,"
Again we find in words divine,
That death's the lot of all man-kind,
Thus: 'tis appointed unto man,
To yield to death's relentless hand.
But lo! the Lord Jehovah cries,

'Tis nothing but the clay that dies;
The soul shall live through endless day,
While all things else shall pass away.
And after cold grim monster death,
Shall force us to yield up our breath,
Our lot of bliss or woe will be,
Throughout immense eternity!
Eternity, oh! that dreaded sound!
How vast it is, and how profound!
The soul once damned is never free,
From fi'ry wrath and misery!
But if we live with Christ our guide,
The stormy skies we'll all outride,
By angels then we will be borne,
Up to that bright and heav'nly throne,
There live at peace with God on high.
Where pain's unknown and tears are dry,
And praise His name forever more.
With friends, dear friends who've gone before,
Now hark! and listen to the word,
Christ spoke, and His disciples heard,
Keep my commands and follow me,
And death you'll never taste or see,
For blessed are the pure in heart,
Their God they'll see and ne'er depart,
From Him nor His unceasing love;
But ever live with Him above.

— *F. Willis Keene*

Lines to Little Ella on Having Her Hair Cut

On Bell Farm lives little Ella Keene,
Alias Ann Bacon;
She thinks she has great troubles seen,
And feels herself forsaken.
The cause of which, some months ago,
Her hair was cut so close,
That now the curls she cannot show,
Of which she used to boast.

She mourns and sighs by night and day,
And sobs and cries withal,
For that blest pear that's taken away,
Which was her all in all.

But why should "Ann" now mourn for that
Which time can soon restore?
And in her fav'rite color, black,
Much prettier than before.

So Ann weep not, weep not I say,
Your hair will shortly grow;
And 'round your neck and shoulders play,
And make a graceful show.

— *F. Willis Keene*

Acrostic for Cousin Bettie

These lines Cousin Bettie, I write for you,
On kindred love, most kind and true,
Could I but see thee -- shake thy hand,
On native soil, Virginia's land,
Unknown my joy would be;
Sweet thoughts would thro' my mind pervade,
Intrinsic bliss would be displayed,
Ne'er thought or dreamed by thee.
But, long the road, that 'tween us lies,
Eternal mountains upward rise,
To shut thee from my view;
The placid streams do run between,
In beauty, forests intervene,
Elysian prairies too.
Despite of all, soon may we meet,
Kindly to each other greet;
Enjoy true kindred mirth,
Ecstatic may your pleasure be,
No strife, but sweet felicity,
Ever, upon this earth.

— *F. Willis Keene*

ON LIFE

To Delinquents

Delinquents, pay the Editors,
They hate to dun as other men;
For truly they are creditors,
Who greatly hate, their friends offend,
Methinks you would, if you'd reflect,
Pay up at once, and not neglect.

Consider first their great expense,
And then their toil both night and day.
Then surely 'twould not cause offense
To humbly ask this debt to pay;
However small the bill may be
They will receive it thankfully.

It matters not how warm nor cold,
The Editor will ne'er refuse
The foreign, sheets to all unfold,
And type you all important news;
The foreign and domestic too,
They never fail to send to you.

Yes, all important current news
We get via of the printing press,
Which we in leisure can peruse;
This fact none can forbear confess;
Yet, there are some delinquents still
Will forego to pay their bill.

Come, all who now are debtors thus,
Haul out some of those "rusty dimes,"
And place them in the printer's "puss,"
For hard, indeed, hard are the times;
Then ne'er again delinquents be,

As for myself, I frankly say,
And thus have thought from early youth,
This bill should be the first you pay;
'Tis thus I think, and speak forsooth.
Reflect, the printer's toils each day,
Go settle up without delay.

— *F. Willis Keene*

The Creation of the World

In the beginning of this world,
God made the heaven and earth;
And all therein, and it was good
Then gave to man his birth.

Now earth was void and without form
And chaos reigned instead;
Then were the waters of the deep,
With darkness overspread.

And gently o'er the water's face,
The Holy Spirit steered;
When this command, "Let there be light",
Was made, and light appeared.

And God beheld the light be made
And said that it was good;
Its purpose to the new-born world,
Was quickly understood.

The darkness then by his command,
Divided from the light;
The light He gave the name of day,
The darkness that of night.

The morning and the evening past,
The first day's work complete;
Now, "Let there be a firmament",
We learn that God did speak.

And there appeared a firmament,
A firmament of love;
Which did the waters from beneath,
Divide from those above.

The firmament which then appeared,
By Him a name was given;
And now we learn from Holy Writ,
The name He gave was Heaven.

From Bible source we also learn,
This closed the Second day;
On which this work so great was done
And it had passed away.
The third day's work was next begun
When by Supreme Command;
The waters formed in ocean beds,
And there appeared dry land,

Which God the Father said was good,
And earth its name should be;
The waters that were nameless then,
He give the name of Sea.

Then said He, "Let the earth bring forth,
The fruit tree, herb and grass;
Each one to yield its like of fruit,"
Which also came to pass.

The fourth day next was ushered in
On which new lights appeared;
Bright-shining in the upper realm,
By God's own Sovereign Word.

The day and night now in divide,
These lights were His designs;
For days, for years and Seasons too,
And also were for signs.

Two of these lights, the Sun and Moon,
He made and called great lights;
The Sun was made to rule the days,
The moon to rule the nights.

The stars that also make the skies,
So cheerful and so bright;
Were put in place by wise design,
Which changed the gloom of night.

This work so marvelous and grand,
These lights of priceless worth;
Placed in the vaulted skies above
To warm and light the earth.

The fourth day now was in the past,
The fifth day was on time;
When wonder work was going on
Creative and sublime.

The waters of the mighty deep,
The vast expanse of land;
Brought forth all living, creeping things,
According to Command.

He made the whales and fish that swim,
The fowls and birds that fly;
And this injunction gave to them,
"Be fruitful, multiply".

"And fill the waters in the seas,
Increase in all the earth;"

Which was obeyed in every case,
By means of magic birth.

This now completes the fifth day's work,
The sixth was next begun;
When Holy wisdom, deep, profound,
Shone forth in what was done.

Now, "Let the earth bring forth, said He,
And after his own kind;
The living creature, creeping things,
Cattle and beasts combined.

The next command, "Let's make a man",
Was also soon obeyed;
When wonderfully strange this man,
From common dust was made.

Then God into his nostrils breathed,
The breath that gave him life;
When man became a living soul,
Unmarred by sin or strife.

He also caused a sleep profound,
To fall upon this man;
Took out a rib, closed up the flesh,
According to His plan.

Cosmopolite
— *F. Willis Keene*

Campaign Song for Stephen Douglas

Tune - Love and Cider

Hurrah, hurrah ye patriot band,
Come join us in the chorus,
And raise your voices for the man,
Whose flag now waves before us;
His name now floats upon the breeze,
While we in acclamation,
Give cheers united for the man,
The pride of this great nation.
Chorus -Come rally Union men,
Come rally Union men,
Come rally round our chieftain bold,
And victory we will win.

Come Union lovers one and all,
At once prepare for action,
To route "Old Abe's desponding clan,
And quell the Danite faction.
yes, boldly gird your armor on,
And now the work begin,
With courage to the rescue come,
And victory we'll win.
Chorus - Come rally Union men &c.

Each day we hear from north and south,
Of "sinners" being changed
From error, and the sable band
With which they long have ranged;
Soon as their eyes beheld the truth,
And minds conceive the right,
They side at once with "Stephen A,"
And boldly meet the fight.
Chorus - Come rally Union men &c.

Come rally for our Western sage,
And gallant statesman too,
A man whose every move and act
Is firm, united, true,
And man whose lofty intellect,
And eloquence so bright,
Subdued the champion of the north,
And put his crew to flight.
Chorus - Come rally Union men &c.

A man whose firm intrepid look,
And words of power and weight,
Defies the vanquished Seceders,
And neophytes create.
Non-intervention is his cry,
The Union is his text,
At which the Abolition band
Became incensed and vexed.
Chorus - Come rally Union men, &c.

Hurrah, hurrah, for our men,
With Union hearts elate,
Next Fall he'd be the champion,
And guide the ship of state.
From east, from west, from north and south,
Come Union lovers all,
And rally round the Union man,
And vote for him next Fall.

F.W.K. August 2, 1860

— *F. Willis Keene*

Hurrah for Douglas

Tune - Wait for the Wagon

Another presidential strife
And campaign is at hand,
Four candidates I believe are out,
Whose names float o'er the land;
And hence the question will arise
Which man will be elected?
To which the Union man can say
The one which we've selected.
Chorus - Wait 'till November,
Wait 'till November,
Wait 'till November
And bold STEVE will guide the ship.

The man who holds the Union dear,
In every word and action;
Whose courage true and manly course
Defies the Danite faction:
Whose firm position, steadfast, bold,
And words of power true,
Will put to flight before next fall,
The "mauler's" little crew.
Chorus - Wait 'till November, &c.

And leave behind quite out of sight,
And out of mind, John Bell.
While all will plainly hear the clapper,
Strike loud his funeral knell.
And "Stephen A." will take his seat.
The head of this great nation,
And meet with cheers from north and south
In welcome acceptation.
Chorus - So wait 'till November, &c.

So Union lovers, all hurrah!
With hearts and mind elate;
Our "little" man will be next March
Placed at the helm of state.
For now's the time a Union man,
A statesman true we need;
And "Stephen" is the very "boy"
Our ship can safely lead.
Chorus - So wait 'till November, &c.

A gallant man, a chieftain true,
A patriot and a sage,
A hero with master mind
Can check disunion's rage.
Affairs at present plainly show,
While storms and tempest wave,
The Douglas is the only man
The Union can save
Chorus - So wait 'till November, &c.

— *F. Willis Keene*

The Week

Sunday is the holy day,
God blessed and sanctified,
On which there should no work be done
He plainly specified.

Monday next we always find,
To never fail come in,
Which is the day for every one,
There daily work begin.

Tuesday too will ne'er forbear,
To be the next in turn;
When many persons are at work,
Their daily bread to earn.

Wednesday next we find appears,
When work we should resume,
Without a murmur or a word,
Also without a gloom.

Thursday always follows too,
Without the slightest doubt;
Be all assured, you'll never found,
This day to be left out.

Friday in succession comes,
Again our tasks we seek,
And this we find will prove to be,
The sixth day of the week.

Saturday next, is the day,
That proves to be the last;
When work is o'er, and day gone by,
We find the week is past.

— *F. Willis Keene*

Sooner or Later

Sooner or later
Their reign here shall end
And the kingdom that has grounded you
Surely will bend
For their grip's been tight forever
And the heavy chains they won't release
But faith can win your battle dear
Sending you to bondage free
There'll be no price for the air you breath
And your children shall run free
When all the angels dance
Upon the grass so green
So if the chains are tight – surrender not
Freedom will come calling one day
Though it's not the life you sought
Heaven will find you anyway
'Cause sooner or later
Their reign here shall end
And the kingdom that has grounded you
Surely will bend
So take your wings and fly
To another world
Until the day the angels come
When shackles are unfurled
And the war is finally won

— *Todd Keene*

Henry VIII

So you danced at Piccadilly
And the circus played just for you
And the view's been just fine up there
From the monarch's private pew
The royal life becomes you dear
An oyster plucked from shallow sea
A gem upon the royal crown
On display for all to see
So partake the rarified air
Breath it in whilst favor is upon you
So have your dance in Piccadilly
Where the circus plays just for you
Have your tea in the Royal Mews
With the King you can't refuse
But when the fools and jesters call
Surely you must answer
Their hollow, acrid drawl
Yea, savor the sun in its shining moments
Sing of love, loud and true
But know that the crush shall come
When H exacts his price
What's done is done
And it's your head he's coming for
Your blood must flow, through and through
But never from the royal H
The one with blood so blue

— *Todd Keene*

Chelsea Bridge

The Chelsea Bridge closed early this day
Her majesty exiled
From ought-two she'd held true
From the east and west they'd filed
The watchman said she'd give way at three
Her years of service through
Succumbed to loins tired and frayed
From lorries and the noble steeds
The years of weight had tolled
Forgotten is the faithful she
By those who'd crossed the raging sea
But the lives she claimed as girders gave
Won't pass this way again
From the Vicar to the Magistrate
The souls to save the Lord they prayed
With sullen brows they wondered
How to break the wretched news
The flags shalln't fly at full today
Rather, bells shall ring thirty and three
For the lives she'd taken, adrift upon the bay
Farewell to thee they'll sadly sing
For the tragedy she'd bring
They'll measure the cost in the lives she lost
Her decades of safe passage tossed
Once esteemed and lauded she
Her grander moments recalled by few
In time they'll ask, if you only knew
That Chelsea once was might and true
In her year of one o' two

— *Todd Keene*

Florida

A gentle mist whispers from the tide
Life starts on the island
Timid chameleons scatter and hid
Miniature footprints softly break the sand
Docile rays of sunlight emerge
Water expectantly glistens
Restless seagulls gallantly flourish
Triumphant sounds for those who listen
The ocean carries a relentless pulse
Of water, shells and sand
Nothing compares with the limitless Gulf
Or the beauty of this land

— *Todd Keene*

Compromise

Love looks past the eyes
Concern is sullen fear disguised
Hope is the redeemer of tomorrows
Anxiety brings forth remised sorrows
But change can happen
The novel rewritten
And out of the darkness struts Compromise
So relieve the power
And change the few
Give the promise of life
Truly see another's rage
Then our problems are not a book, but a page

— *Todd Keene*

Camelot

This isn't Camelot
You've changed the plot
You've not a lot to say
I'm fairly sure
That what you are
Is changing by the day
What's happened here
What is it, dear?
What's sent you on your way
The questions fly
No thoughts subside
No answers come today
This silly dance
This flawed romance
Nothing but charade

— *Todd Keene*

A Trip to the Mountain (tune – O'Susanna)

Written for a friend on his visit to the Bull-run mountain

Some time ago I made a trip
Which now I will relate
It happened on a mountain top
In old Virginia State
'Tis sweet pleasure
The mountain top to see
It fills my soul with happiness
And heart with ecstasy
I left my home one Sunday morn
In company with a friend
And to the Bull-run mountain went
And there the day did spend
'Tis sweet pleasure
The mountain top to see
It fills my soul with happiness
And heart with ecstasy
It was my fortune there to see
Young ladies of all kind
And one of them I do aver
Appeared to me divine
Her charming curls of ravel hair
Which do her shoulders deck
Hung wavingly and gracefully
Around her pretty neck
Indeed she is divinely fair
Her charms I do admire
Could I but say that she was mine
Tis all I could desire
'Tis sweet pleasure
The mountain top to see
It fills my soul with happiness
And heart with ecstasy

Bell Farm Loudowm Co. Va. July 19, 1858

— *F. Willis Keene*

The Unlucky Daguerreotypist

A peasant boy near seventh gate
Once formed within his mind
That he would learn to likeness take
And leave the farm behind
So on to Middlebury he went
With heart and mind elate
And there two weeks I believe he spent
In learning to likeness take
Poor little fellow
Alas! he was too late
The art was then in every town
Throughout Virginia State
From thence to home he did repair
Supplied with plates and cases
Assuring them all if the weather be fair
He'd take punctilious faces
His room he chose, his camera set
His plates he rubbed to brighten
Then quoth he, now I'm ready, I'll bet
Your pocketbooks to lighten
The people came in after a while
To have their pretties taken
He sang some songs to make them smile
Their impressions to awaken
At home three weeks I believe he spent
Then, by solicitation
To a neighbor's house he went
To practice his profession
And there a day or so he stayed
His board he just did clear
Then up his mind he firmly made
To Salem he'd repair
A few days only there he spent

Finding poor reception
In consequence thereof he went
Straightway to Markham station
But sad to say when there he got
He felt like one forsaken
For all there said that they did not
Want any pictures taken
Then said he, I'll not further roam
My board I just can pay
So then pap's cart he took for home
And there resolved to stay
Poor little fellow
Alas he was too late
The art was then in every town
Throughout Virginia State.

Bell Farm, Loudown Co. Va. July 21, 1858

— *F. Willis Keene*

Communicated

Mr. Editor—Sir:
By ubiquitary sanction, and Omniscient ratification, I approximate this lymphatic sheet, pursuant to a previous avowed design, to rehearse a few items, in conjunction with a delineated description of this section of the great occident.

Allow me in the preface or exordium of this illogical, laconic missive, to interlace that health, the great divine favor and sublunary benison, emanating from the great I AM, is a pervading theme throughout this section of country.

This village (Groveland), is an extremely healthful location. The surrounding vicinity is quite level, and the land is very rich—the soil is about two feet and a half in depth and abundantly lucrative. The farmers are now in the midst of their wheat harvest, but the yield of the fall sowing will not be very exorbitant; as the winter was not at all favorable to it. The spring sowing will yield more abundantly, owing to the mildness of the spring. Sowing wheat in the spring of the year may appear ludicrous to Loudoun farmers; the but principal portion of the wheat crops here are of that description, and ecumenically surpass the fall sowing. Corn is looking well, and growing finely, and bids fair for an abundant harvest.

Corn is not thinned here as in Virginia; it produces well with five and six stalks in a hill. It is a common thing here for farmers to raise 60 and 75 bushels of corn to the acre, which is equivalent to 12 and 15 barrels per acre. Fruit in this section of the country is tolerably good; but does not compare with that of Old Virginia. Apple orchards are all young—I have not seen an old orchard yet. I have been informed that the trees here will not live to the age that they do in Virginia, that the longevity of the fruit trees in general is short. Cherries are principally morel or sour cherries. The sweet black-hearts and large sweet red-hearts are very scarce, I have not seen any yet. Pears and other fruits are tolerably scarce. Timber is quite plentiful in this immediate scope of country. Peoria quotations for grain on the 29th June, were as follows: Corn in the ear 60 a 61c.; shelled 62 a 63c. Wheat good quality of spring 80 a 85c.; winter 90 a 100c. Oats 35c. Rye 65c. Barley 45 a 60c.

The beautiful and flourishing city of Peoria is situated on the western bank of the Illinois River (or Peoria Lake), about 7 miles distant from this place, in a northwestern direction. I am informed that 10 years ago it only claimed 4,000 inhabitants, and now it numbers about 30,000. Business matters there are quite stagnant now to what they hitherto have been; but yet times are moderately progressive, and new buildings are diurnally in progress. Immediately west of the city, there is quite an elevated portion of land called a Bluff, which is handsomely decorated with sundry kinds and variegated wild flowers, grass and beautiful trees, which presents a paradisiacal and sublime aspect viewed from its base or the city. And upon ascending to its summit, which is several hundred feet above the level of the lake, and taking an ocular demonstration or optical reconnoiter of the city, which is wholly and clearly to view, and directing the sight up and down the lovely meandering stream for miles, and viewing in the great distance the fields of ripening wheat and growing corn, the observer cannot forbear from saying that nature in its course and bestowals had been rather partial to that immediate section, and lavished a great degree of loveliness and splendor there, which caused the surrounding country, viewed from the summit of the delectable and floriferous bluff, to be picturesque and magnificent beyond description.

I was one of the vast number present in Peoria on the 4th, and a more pleasant and propitious day for a celebration could not have been desired. The morning rays of Old Sol, who was coursing his way through the arched convex heavens, broke forth resplendently, and deliciously clear and cool, and the heat was not oppressive any time during the day. It was estimated that there were more persons present in the city on that day, than ever before on such an occasion. The morning was saluted with a salvo of thirty-three guns—one for each State. The procession which was elegantly emblazoned and caparisoned, was formed with commendable promptness, and extremely good order was preserved throughout the day. The orator of the day acquitted himself very eloquently. He occupied about three-fourths of an hour in delivering his address, which was well written and quite able. The leading topic of the oration was the Declaration of Independence, its history and bearings upon the past, present, and future of political history. The fire works from the Court House Square in the evening, were, some of them, exceedingly interesting; but many of them proved failures, owing to the fact that the wheels stubbornly refused to revolve. When started even, they would stop, hesitate which way to go, oscillate between two causes, and then settle down into a motionless position again. If it were not for fear of prolixity characterizing my incoherent effusion, I would give you more extended detail; but resting under such magical influence, I will bring these lines to a consummation, by very bluntly subscribing yourself my friend.

F.W.K.

— *F. Willis Keene*

A Charade

My first is the initial of the name
Of a brave general known to fame
And now my friend awake from slumber
My second is a decimal number.
And my third now then will find
To be a novel of English kind
My fourth will prove without a doubt
A word of number study it out.
My whole you'll find to be a word
That proves to be an active verb.
This I submit to anyone
To solve, and give the answer soon.

Bell Farms, Loudoun Co. Virginia
July 8, 1858

— *F. Willis Keene*

Hard Times

Hard times, hard times is sounded everywhere
And harder times are coming, the most of people fear
This is the theme in parlor, and in secluded dell
In fact we all are troubled our countenance tell.
But we should not encourage such thoughts or conversation
But strive to make times easy and shun this deflation
The cause of this great pressure is marked by suspending banks
And crops failing generally 'gainst which we are contending
One thing should cheer us onward to hope or times better
That this is the banks suspended, are passing out the dimes
And we are told by persons of judgment more mature
Good crops will mark the future and make us all secure.

Bell Farm, Loudoun Co. Virginia
July 19, 1858

— *F. Willis Keene*

Religion

Religion! oh that blissful thought,
Of pure and fathomless delight;
Thy beams doth fill the soul with joy;
Oh! thou cherub heavenly bright.
Thy force Religion, death disarms,
Thy blest effulgence can dispel,
The clouds of grief induced by sin,
And all the dreaded fears of hell!
Now view Religion, and her charms,
Dispersing heavenly blessings sweet;
From her fair eyes, thou brilliant rays,
Are shining forth, with joy replete.
Thou canst impart ethereal light,
Give life divine and lasting bliss,
Unveil our eyes, and open to view,
Scenes of eternal happiness.
And all our sorrow, despair and doom;
Thy mighty force can soon erase,
Put sunshine in the place of gloom
And fill our souls with heav'nly grace.

— *F. Willis Keene*

Lines on a Fillmore and Donelson Barbecue which took place on October 1, 1856

Fillmore and Donelson Barbecue
The time fixed on for that event.
Has come and passed away;
And there the day I happily spent.
The scene I'll now portray
First in the rostrum to defend,
Our great American cause
Was S.G. Stewart of Fairfax clime
Who met with great applause.
He said affairs at present showed,
While storms and tempests wave;
That Fillmore was the only man
The Union now could save.
Then W.H. Delaney next,
Before us did appear;
With Fillmore for his glorious text,
　　　　Spoke boldly without fear.
Against old Buck he warned us all
　　　　And said he was unsound;
And if selected president,
For Cuba he was bound.
Much more he said,
Let this suffice
　　　　His speech much admired;
And with the cheers on either side,
　　　　He calmly then retired.
H.W. Thomas then arose,
　　　　Amid cheers and great applause,
Unto the crowd was introduced,
　　　　A Whig for our cause.
A patriotic speech he made
　　　　And said to all remember,

And not forget -- be up awake,
          And rally next November.
B.H. Shackleford then appeared;
          And with uplifted hand,
Zealously, yet calmly spoke
          Of danger in our land.
He said to all, come rally now,
          A statesman true we need;
And Fillmore is the only man
          Our ship can safely lead.

Bell Farm, Loudoun County Virginia

— *F. Willis Keene*

On the Death of a Faithful Dog, Lion

Grim monster death with icy grasp.
I'm sorry now to say.
Hath seized upon poor Lion's frame
And summoned him away.
So now he is forever gone
No more we'll see his face;
He never can return again,
To join the canine race.
Though Lion now is dead and gone
His name he leaves behind.
Which loudly speaks and says he was
The best of all his kind.
In hunting squirrels and treeing them,
And chasing of the rabbit,
He occupied most all his time,
Which proved to be his habit.
I now assert a better dog,
You'll never, never find,
Through life his acts spoke him to be,
True, gentle, good and kind.
A few weeks prior to his death,
We gave poor Lion away.
His master new he did not like.
And would not with him stay.
But quickly he returned to us
Crippled, maimed and poor,
With sundry howls and frequent groans,
He died close by our door.

Bell Farm, Loudoun Co., Va.
July 22, 1858

— *F. Willis Keene*

On the Death of Little Unie

My father owned a faithful pet,
Classed with the canine race;
Her size was small but yet well set,
With crocus colored face.
Her name was I'll now proceed to tell,
Although it was quite funny
Yet all who knew her, knew full well
Her name was little Unie.
In guarding 'round her master's house
She had no parallel;
To kill the rat, and catch the mouse
No dog could her excel.
With her I've roamed the hills and dales
To hunt the hare and squirrel;
But by the hand of death at last
She's hurried from this world.
A better little hunting dog
Was never known to be,
A better dog to guard the house,
I never expect to see.
A faithful pet she was indeed
So all did frankly say;
Thus onward did her good traits lead
To equal "old dog Tray".

Bell Farm, Loudoun Co., Va.
July 22, 1858

— *F. Willis Keene*

On the Death of Old Pomp

On Friday, the eighteenth day of June,
In the year of 'fifty-eight,
I'm sorry to say for poor old Pomp
Death proved to be her fate.
So now she's gone forever gone!
And left her son (Taylor) behind.
Alone to sigh, to weep and mourn,
And consolation find.
She's gone to ne'er return
To join the canine race
On guard around her master's house
Or view poor Taylor's face
A few days prior to her death
Refused she did to eat,
And wandered in the field alone
Through the oppressive heat;
But poor old Pomp was forc'd at last,
To find herself a bed;
Beneath an apple tree nearby;
In which, she was found dead.

Bell Farm, Loudoun Co., Va.
July 22, 1858

— *F. Willis Keene*

On Parting

When friends, true friends, are called to part,
To say the word farewell;
The sorrow that pervades the heart,
Is hard for words to tell.
Experience now, has taught me thus,
The parting pang to know;
By tracing these imperfect lines,
will show.
My lot has been to part from friends,
And kindred near and dear;
And some of them have gone above,
No more to greet them here.
But still I hope my lot may be,
To meet those friends once more,
To greet them yon above the sky--
On Canaan's happy shore.
We have assurance from that King,
Whose mansion's in the sky,
That He will consolation give,
And all our wants supply.
If we will turn from things terrain,
From worldly ways be risen;
And lay up treasure not on Earth,
But treasure up in Heaven.
And when my days on Earth are o'er,
And moment comes to die;
May Christ receive me to His fold,
To dwell with Him on high.

Bell Farm, Loudoun Co., Va.
July 24, 1858

— *F. Willis Keene*

Johnny Keene, Alias Trout, Alias Krout

I well do know a little boy,
Who is withal quite spry;
He's seen in summer to decoy,
The bee and butterfly.
The junebug can't his vengeance shun,
Nor mouse escape his power;
The bumblebee he hills through fun,
While sitting on the flower.
This little fellow's proper name,
Is known as Johnny K;
Though he is even found ashame,
To own it in his play.
But, when you call his other name,
Which I believe is "Trout,"
He'll quickly answer to the same,
And come, if near about.
But when we have a long hot day,
He will without a doubt,
Perspire freely from his play;
And say'un sour Krout.
Though such is apt to be the case,
With every little lad;
But fear not "Krout", time will erase,
And make you merry glad.
Hence originates the name,
Of little "Sour Krout,"
Which I do fear, will him defame,
If it should e'er get out.
So "Krout" your name you ought to change,
Before it's widely known;
And in a better sphere to range,
And rise to some renown.
Now "Trout" don't let this stop your play,

In yard nor in the house —
Although I feel quite frank to say,
"I've taken down your "Souse."

Bell Farm, Loudoun Co., Va.
September 2, 1858

— *F. Willis Keene*

On Home

One may travel far and long
All o'er the world may roam,
But still he'll hum the poet's song
"There is no place like home."
And with your friends and kindred kind,
Where favors may be shown,
Let me assert you'll these not find,
A place to you like home.

Bell Farm, Loudoun Co., Va.
July 24, 1858

— *F. Willis Keene*

What is Man That Thou Art Mindful of Him?

All nature loudly speaks and says,
That thou art all in all O, Lord;
Into existence all things crowd,
In strict obedience to thy word.
Now, when we view the great deep sea,
And then behold the mother land,
We see the mighty works of God.
Compared to this then what is man?
The forest tree, the spire of grass,
All living things of sea and land,
Are in the power of the Lord,
And live or die at His command.
Next view the sun, the moon and stars,
And even minute grains of sand;
All of which by Him were made,
Compared to this, then what is man?
And yet He deigns to notice,
The weak and frail machine,
Tho wonderfully wrought of clay;
He springeth up like spires of grass,
Soon to live and soon to pass,
Poor sinful man! how nearly naught,
Subject to pain and sorrow fraught,
He's in our midst alive today,
And alas! he's gone tomorrow.

— *F. Willis Keene*

Heaven

Heaven! a land of pure delight,
Where endless day excludes the night,
And pleasures reign supreme,
Where Father, Son and Holy Ghost,
And angels, from that might host,
And all is calm, serene.
Where gentle streams of love do flow,
To banish all misery and woe;
In that sweet home above,
Dwelling in the bright happy land,
Singing songs of eternal love,
And living at His right hand.

— *F. Willis Keene*

The Groveland Bee

My poor little goose quills up I take
To see if I can't some verses make
Submitting them as all will see
Expressly for the Groveland Bee
Which will in size and style compete
Appear in Groveland once a week
Each Wednesday night be read aloud
To the Mite society crowd
A journal got up with design
To show the power of each mind
Also to bring each one to bear
And then the eloquence compare
Young ladies who attend the Mite
We welcomely do now invite
To lend their aid be frank and free
To deck and grace the Groveland Bee!

— *F. Willis Keene*

TODD'S CHILDREN'S POETRY

Swimming

Watch me sail these open waters!
I'll chart a course without a bother
I'm a pilot brave, with heart of steel
Move aside, as I guide the nautical wheel

I'm fearless and noble, a force of which to be reckoned
Beware ye straying vessel, when it's I who beckons!
Ahoy yon maiden, allow this ship to pass!
Says I the captain, to the wayward, seafaring lass

Alas, the wind has changed
And the current has sent me alee
Drat the dreaded eddy!
For it's the shore that calls to me

But the sea shall call again tomorrow
And the gulls will prattle and sing
And I shall float a thousand ideas
As mommy affixes my water wings

— *Todd Keene*

Fire Flies

The night in all its darkness
Conceals the wondrous earth
The trees, the land, the fruited plain
Are lost in its shadowy dearth

Alas how the stars may twinkle,
And the moon pretends to shine
They yield the still night sky
To a sight that's more sublime

Flicker, flicker little flies
With tails all aglow
How I marvel as you float along
A more splendid sight, I do not know!

— *Todd Keene*

The Old Witch

The old witch began to stitch
And sewed the perfect yarn
A tale she said that was
All in her head
And hardly worth a darn
But nevertheless
She confessed
To share it would do no harm

Her purpose it seemed
To scare and to squeam
And do what witches do
So for the good of her kind
She put forth a rhyme
A tale that grew and grew

It was frightful she knew
Like one of her stews
A recipe so sublime
She cackled and howled
And boastfully allowed
It was sure to curdle the mind!

This Halloween
And whenever she deemed
She'd haunt and carry through
A plan so rife
With dreadful strife
Too awful to be true

She'd take one of each
Of households, she'd speak
A child for her very own
It was evil of course
And with slightest remorse
She'd rob the houses through.

She'd steal a one
And sometimes two
To her it was all the same
On a whim she withdrew
The numbers to suit
If kiddies only knew! (cont.)
No screams were heard
From lassies and lads
Her spell was far too great
To momma and dad
It was all too sad
Her thirst would never slake

The moral, she knew
It could happen to you!
So watch yourself and learn
Lock your doors
Do all of your chores
And listen to momma's word

Strangers may seem
To be kindly indeed
But turn your back and run
Stay close to dad
Hold onto his hand
You're precious as morning sun

No witches or ghosts
Will harm you she'd boast
If witches could give a care
So trust in your kind
And be of good mind
You're precious beyond compare!

— *Todd Keene*

Sticky Stuff

What's that sticky stuff
That's on the bottom of your shoe?
It it peanut butter, or tape
Or perhaps even glue?

Is it cream cheese, or mud pies
Or icing from a cake?
Could it be bubble gum
For Heaven's sake?

Is it the tar that lines the streets
When you travel way down south?
Or the stuff that slips out
When you sleep with an open mouth?

What's that sticky stuff
That's on the bottom of your shoe?
It's rather soft and gooey
Oh no! It's that little doggie's doo!

— *Todd Keene*

Little Kitty

Little kitty, soft and cuddly too
Will your mommy miss you
When it's home I go with you?

Would you like a cup of milk
Or niblets to see you through?
Are you comfy in your blanket
In my wagon I've prepared for you?

I like your fuzzy tail
And soggy little nose
In the morning, aren't you lucky?
You're already wearing your clothes!

Just another block now
Until we reach our house
You can run and jump and play there
And even catch a mouse!

I promise I'll be gentle
And take good care of you
We'll have a lifelong friendship
To each other, we shall be true.

— *Todd Keene*

Little Piggy

Little piggy, my bank with belly deep
Your tummy holds a fortune
Of coins that I shall keep

Raise your fancy tail
A squeal a mighty oink
When I drop a brand new keepsake
Into your ever growing tank

Let me always remember
And not forget to thank
Those whose gifts I'll treasure
In my little piggy bank.

— *Todd Keene*

Bees

May I have some honey please?
I kindly asked the bumble bees
"To the clover I will gladly go,"
Said the little drone named Bumble Beau

"Then it's on to the comb for me,
It's there I'll spin your source of glee
Whirl and toil and buzz along
Happy am I when my work is done"

"Would you like a spoonful
Or perhaps even two
To savor this treat I've prepared for you?"

Let's make it one for me and one for thee
Said I to my friend the bumble bee

"Tomorrow I'll visit a rose's bloom!"
Bumble Beau said, then off he zoomed
It's here we'll meet said I to he
As I watched in flight, my bumble bee.

— *Todd Keene*

Mister Rogers

On a stroll down the street named Sesame
Did Mister Rogers go
He skipped along and hopscotched too
And passed a talking tree

He looked about and saw his friends
Big Bird and Elmo, with Barnie and Cookie who
Love to play and learn, and rhyme and spell with you!

He rides the choo-choo once a week
To travel someplace new
But it's always fun to come back home
To his neighbors and families too

To make new friends
That's the adventure!
Said Mister Rogers this day
Won't you be mine?
You're well worth knowing,
I might say!

— *Todd Keene*

Haunted House

My oh my do you see
The goblin behind that tree?
Do you hear the shrilly call
From the bedroom down the hall?
Does your spine get tingly and cold
When the wind blows eerie and bold?
Or are you frightened by the mouse
That lurks about this house?
It's just a way of taunting
Not merely just of haunting
A scary way of teasing
That's really not so pleasing
Fear not the awful louse
That runs this haunted house

— *Todd Keene*

It Must Be Halloween

Oh the actors and portrayers
The charlatans and soothsayers
The jesters in conveyance
Trudging slowly house to house
Little goblins, little mermaids
Candy apples from the Muir place
Lighted pumpkins, frightened young ones
Bats and every spooky thing
Oh the dragons have their slayers
Superheroes have naysayers
Masqueraders and purveyors
Carry with them little dreams
Candy treats and yummy sweets
For little feet that walk the night
Halloween is haunted houses
Witches brew and tangled cobwebs
Painted faces, eerie traces
Of lurking creatures, scary features
Mighty mights and little tykes
Holding baby brother's hand
Little angels dressed as devils
Aren't quite who they seem
It must be Halloween!

— *Todd Keene*

LIFE AS WE KNOW IT

Books

Letters form the words
That form the sentences
On a page

Pages form the chapters
That form the books
That make us sage

It's knowledge that we acquire
When we aspire to read a text

With each new page that's turned
It's fun to wonder
To wonder what is next

What's your favorite tome
Or ode
Or lyric too?

It's the one I've yet to read
For I'm exploring what is new!

— *Todd Keene*

Miscellany

'Tis fast the wheels of time roll around,
And seasons pass away;
And soon will Gabriel's trumpet sound,
To speak the judgment day!

In retrospecting gone by bliss,
And moments spent with thee,
My heart is fill'd with happiness,
And sweet felicity.

For you my feelings warmly flow,
O, may they move your heart;
Replete with love, these lines will show,
You still dwell in this heart.
Of all the nymph's I've ever seen,
Unspeakably, thou are supreme.

— *F. Willis Keene*

Random Thoughts

"The least of nature is more than man can create on his own."

"You can lose weight, but you can't gain a personality."

"The cat wouldn't even drag me in."

"When cooking a steak, there's no need to kill it twice."

"I just shoveled two inches of 'partly cloudy' off the driveway."

— *Todd Keene*

Todd Keene

Standing: Mrs. F. Willis Keene, Minnie Edith Keene, Maude Keene Sallee, F. Willis Keene; Seated: Mabel Keene, Florence Sallee, Mrs. Thomas W. Keene

Minnie Edith Keene, Sarah Keene (at piano)

F. Willis Keene

Todd Keene

Everette Keene (at left), F. Willis Keene

Keene Family Home at 1006 S. Jefferson, Peoria

Index

Todd

About the Authors

F. Willis Keene was born on July 8, 1834 in Loudoun County, Virginia. He began writing poetry at an early age, and his family remarked that he constantly studied the dictionary to find the appropriate words for his poems. As an adult, F. Willis was a friend of the politician Stephen Douglas, and authored campaign songs and tributes in his campaign against Abraham Lincoln. He was a frequent guest in the home of President Millard Fillmore, and his account of one such gathering is told herein. He was also a close friend of the great orator, Robert Ingersoll. Despite Ingersoll's gift for the spoken word, he called upon F. Willis to pen a poem to woo his sweetheart to marry him. It worked! Ingersoll remained married to her until his death, at which time Walt Whitman delivered *his* eulogy. F. Willis passed away on March 20, 1911 at the age of 77.

Todd Keene was born 132 years later in 1962, and gained an appreciation for reading and writing at an early age, learning from his mother Barbara, an elementary school teacher. Perhaps the greatest impetus to write came from his fourth-grade teacher at Highland Elementary School in Cheshire, CT. As she was assigning a writing subject for the class, she called Todd to her desk and discretely asked him to write about any subject he wanted to, that his creativity was inspiring to her. The power of our educators! Todd hasn't stopped writing since, having published technical manuals, award-winning marketing literature (Florida's prestigious Addy Award), and more recently, a poem dedicated to his father Walter's caregivers and to caregivers everywhere. Todd and his wife, Vicky, reside in Michigan and remain very active in their lakefront community.

Made in the USA
Middletown, DE
18 September 2020

19139010R00068